My Sister, My Friend

My Sister, My Friend

Growing up with my sister in West Africa

Written by:

Sophia Blankson

Illustrations by Sophia Opoku

ReadersMagnet, LLC

Dedication

Dedicated to all children throughout the world who are struggling with relationships and whose lives will be touched by reading this book.

Preface

The other day I was watching a talk show about sibling rivalry and my heart felt the pain of the kids who are trying to kill each other just because of the petty differences in them. I had a wonderful childhood experience and I am still very close to my siblings.

When my two daughters were six and four, I started noticing them bickering a lot and drawing apart. I told them they were going to be like friends and not enemies fighting over things. They were to accept their differences and use them to complement their shortcomings. Thank God, it worked. They are now in their forties and they are very close. They spend hours on the telephone every week now that they live apart. They support each other, advice and encourage each other whenever necessary. It is such a delight to watch them interact with each other. I know they will be friends for life.

I believe that putting these thoughts down might help some siblings appreciate each other and give some parents some ideas as to how they can deal with such rivalry before it becomes a bigger problem. Let the children know that it is okay to be different from the other children in birth order, gender, looks, ability to learn and do things, etc. Just let the differences be the bond that will help make the other better too.

Enjoy your siblings. They are the best friends you will ever have if you respect, accept and adore each other for the positive influences they bring to the family.

March 2019

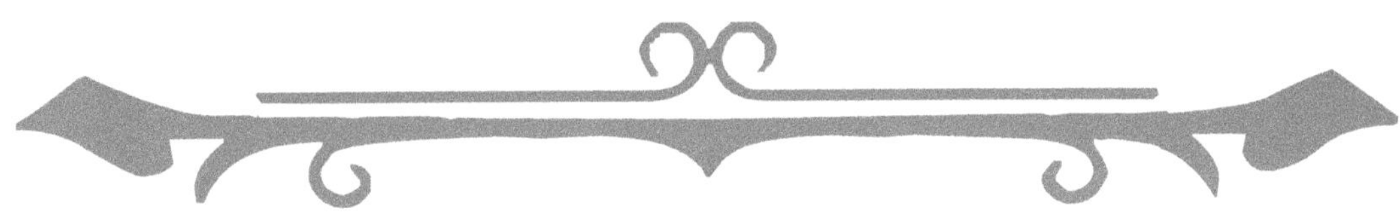

Acknowledgements

I WOULD LIKE TO THANK THE FOLLOWING PEOPLE for making this publication possible:

My sister, Elizabeth Wood-Baisie who was there for me and gave me the example to use in raising my children.

My two daughters, Ekua and Araba who live out the title of this book especially Ekua who helped with the editing of the current edition.

My husband, Charles Blankson, who is truly a friend and a soul mate. His encouragement and help in many many ways and never giving up when some of my dreams were shattered.

My niece, Sophia Opoku, who did the illustrations for this book.

Faye Thomas, Lori Inga, Araba and Ishmael Mensah who helped to transmit the drawings electronically through the editing of the first edition published in 2006.

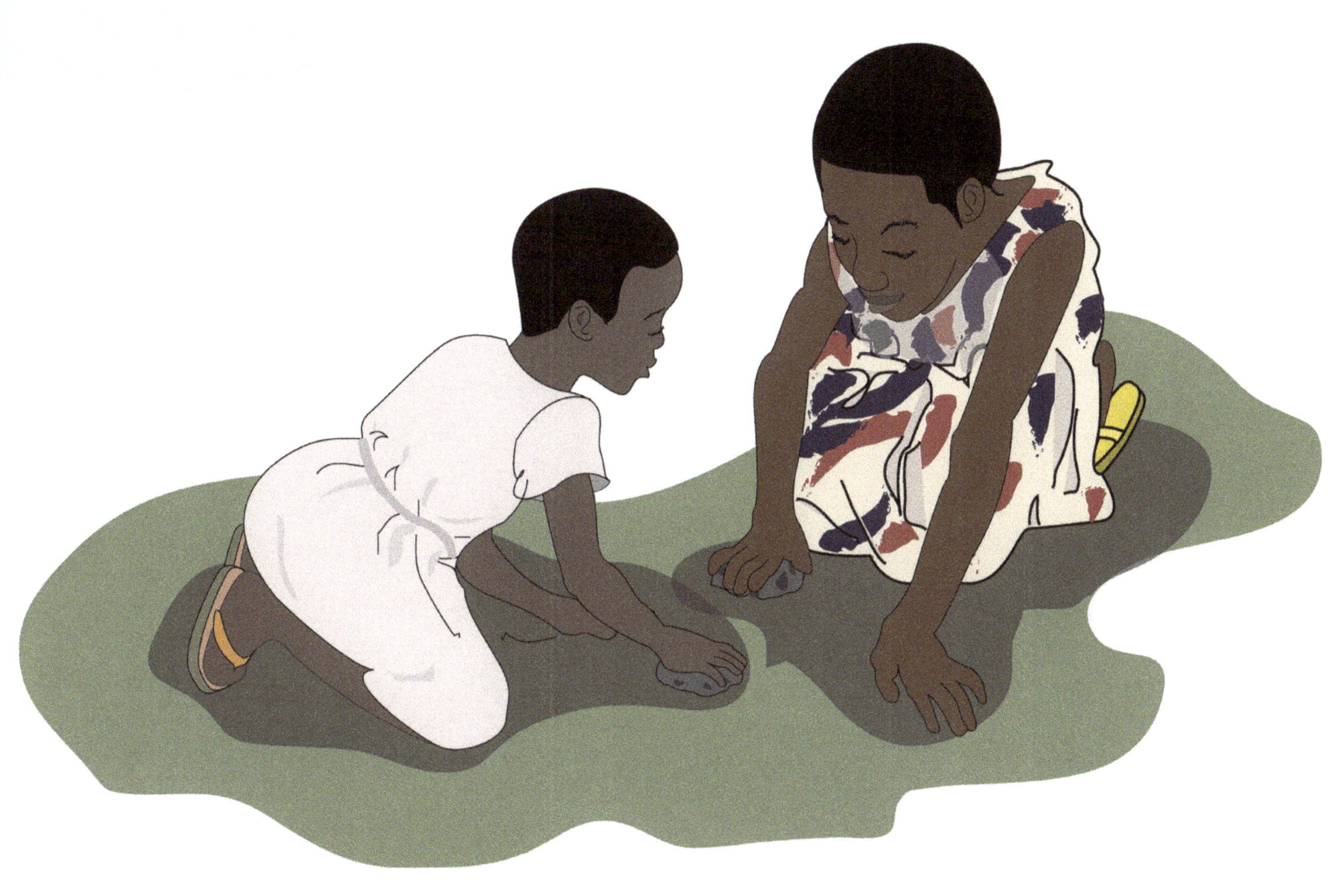

I have a sister. People say we look alike, but we are different in many ways.

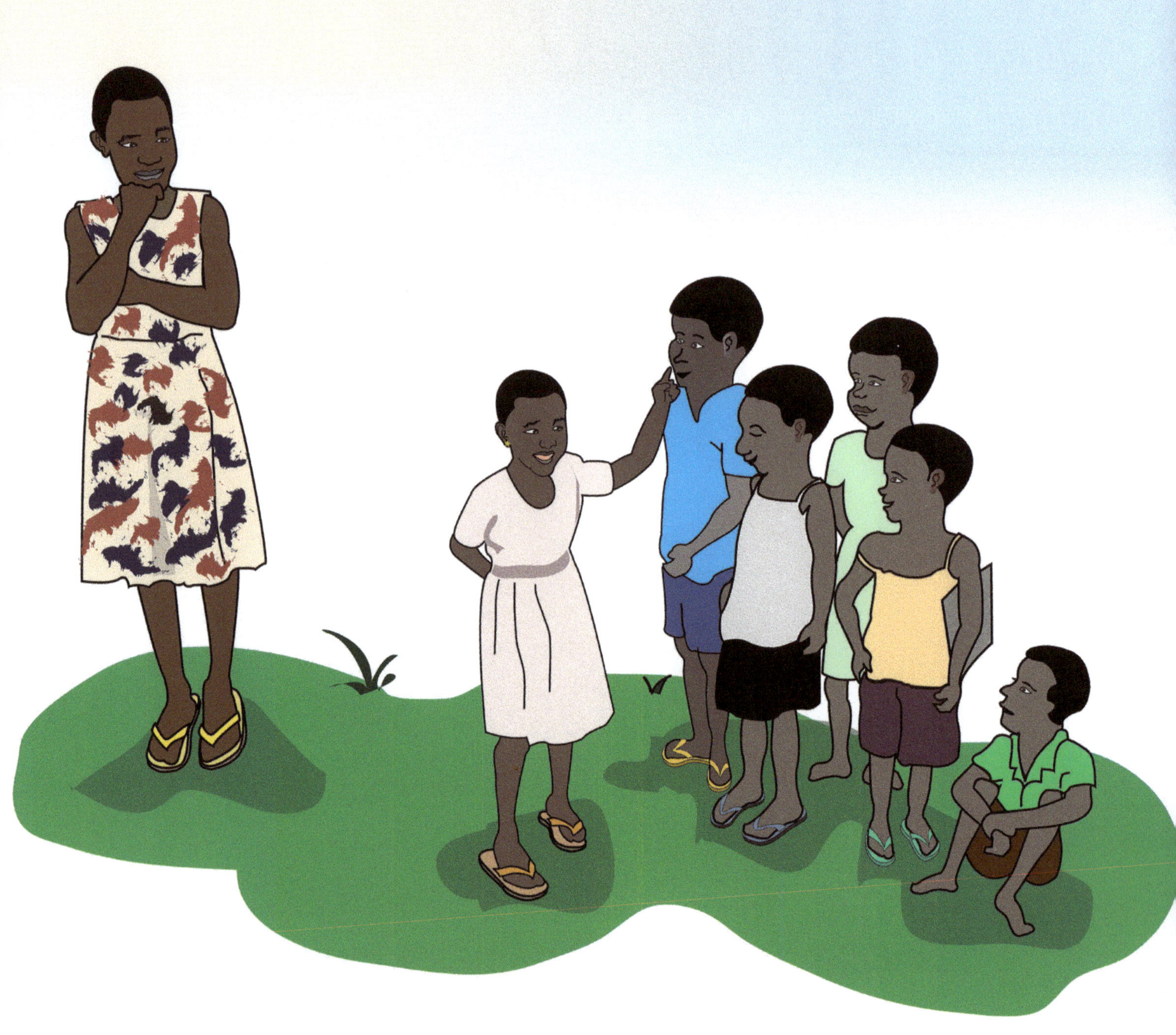

I like to talk, but she is quiet.

So I do all the talking for both of us.

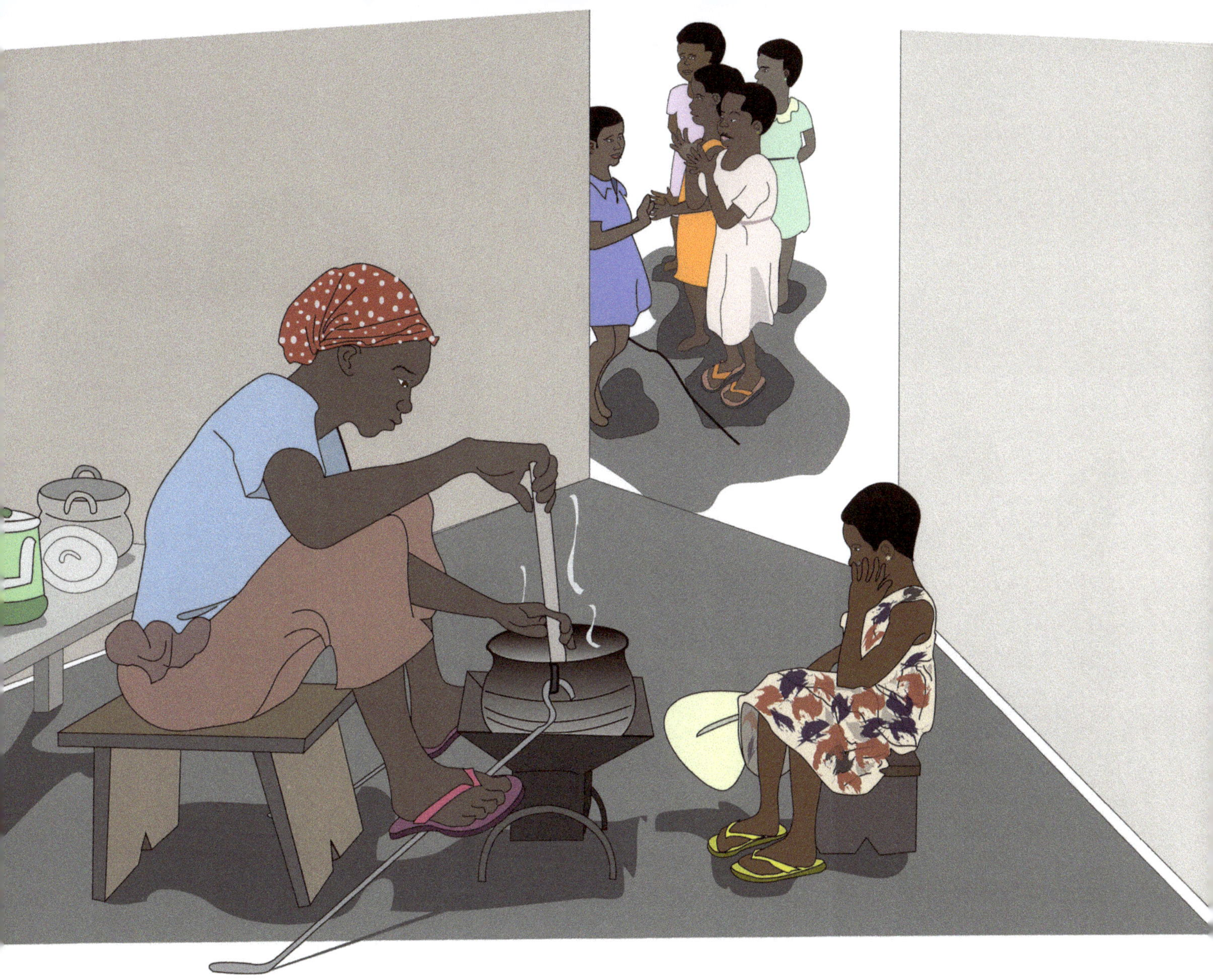

She likes to help Mom in the kitchen,
but I like to play outside.
She does all the helping that
Mom needs from both of us.

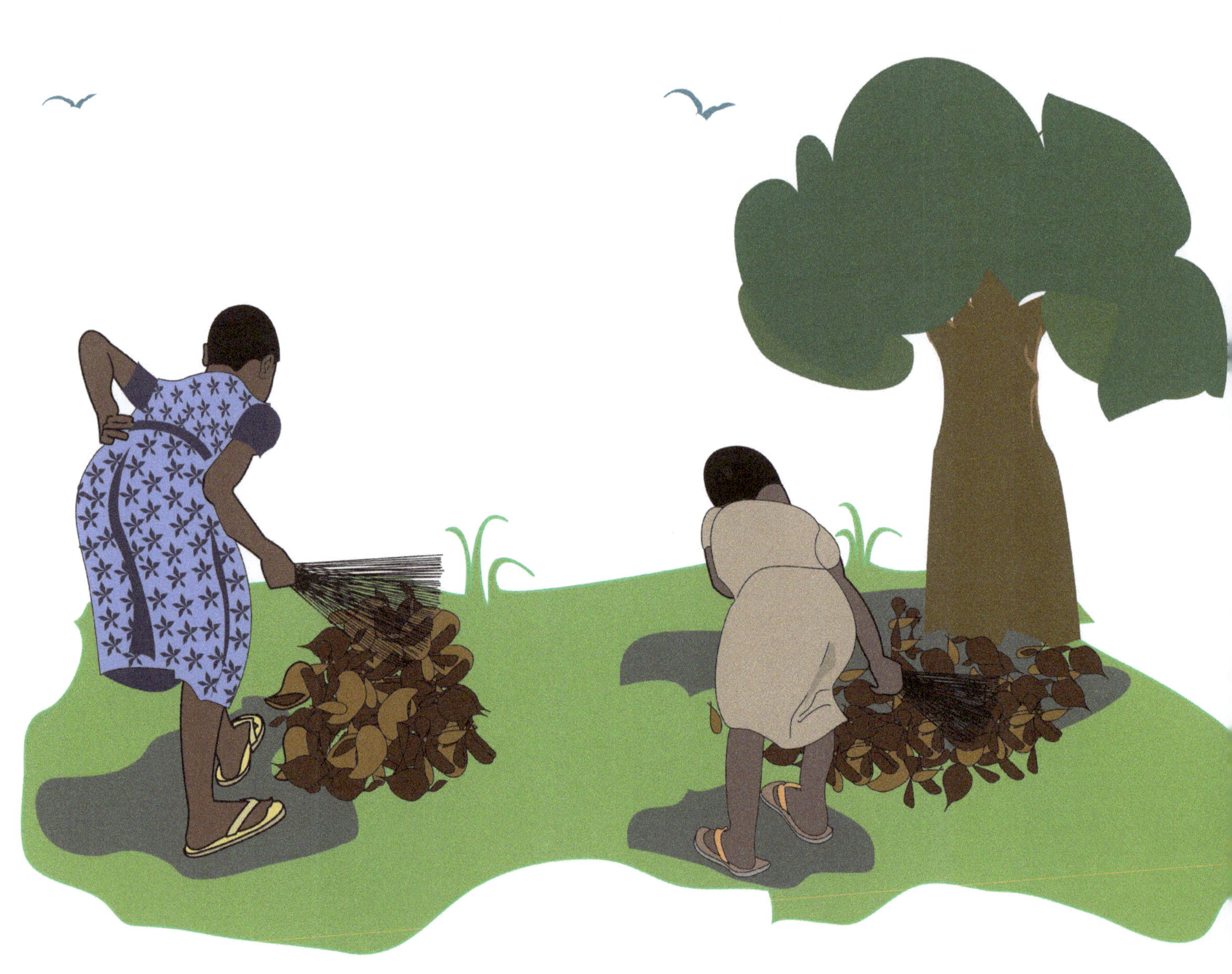

I can't sweep very well, but she
sweeps the yard nicely.
So she does all the sweeping for both of us.

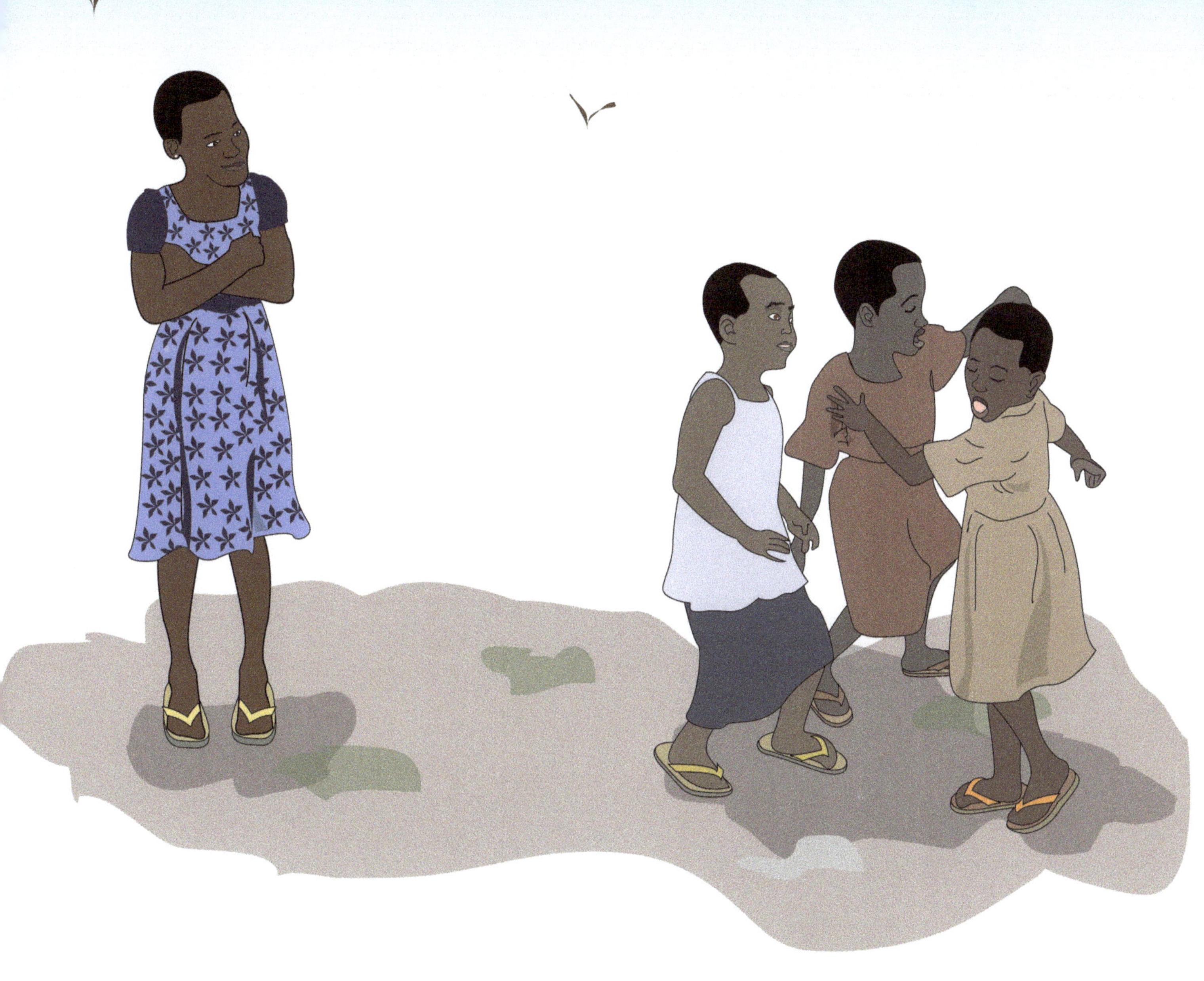

She is shy but I am not shy.
So I make friends for both of us.

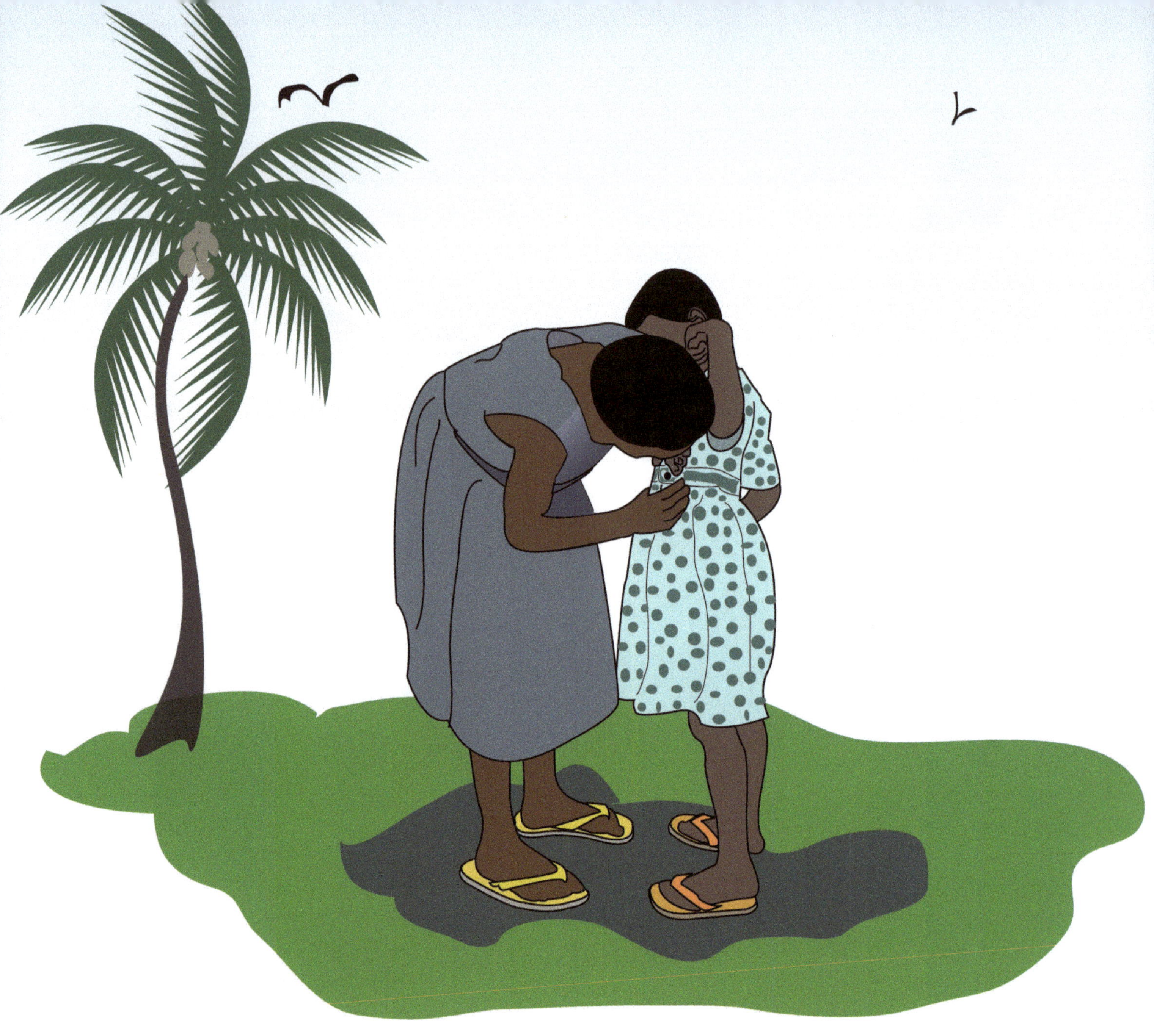

I have a hard time putting on some of my
clothes, but she is good at dressing herself.
So she helps me get dressed when she is finished.

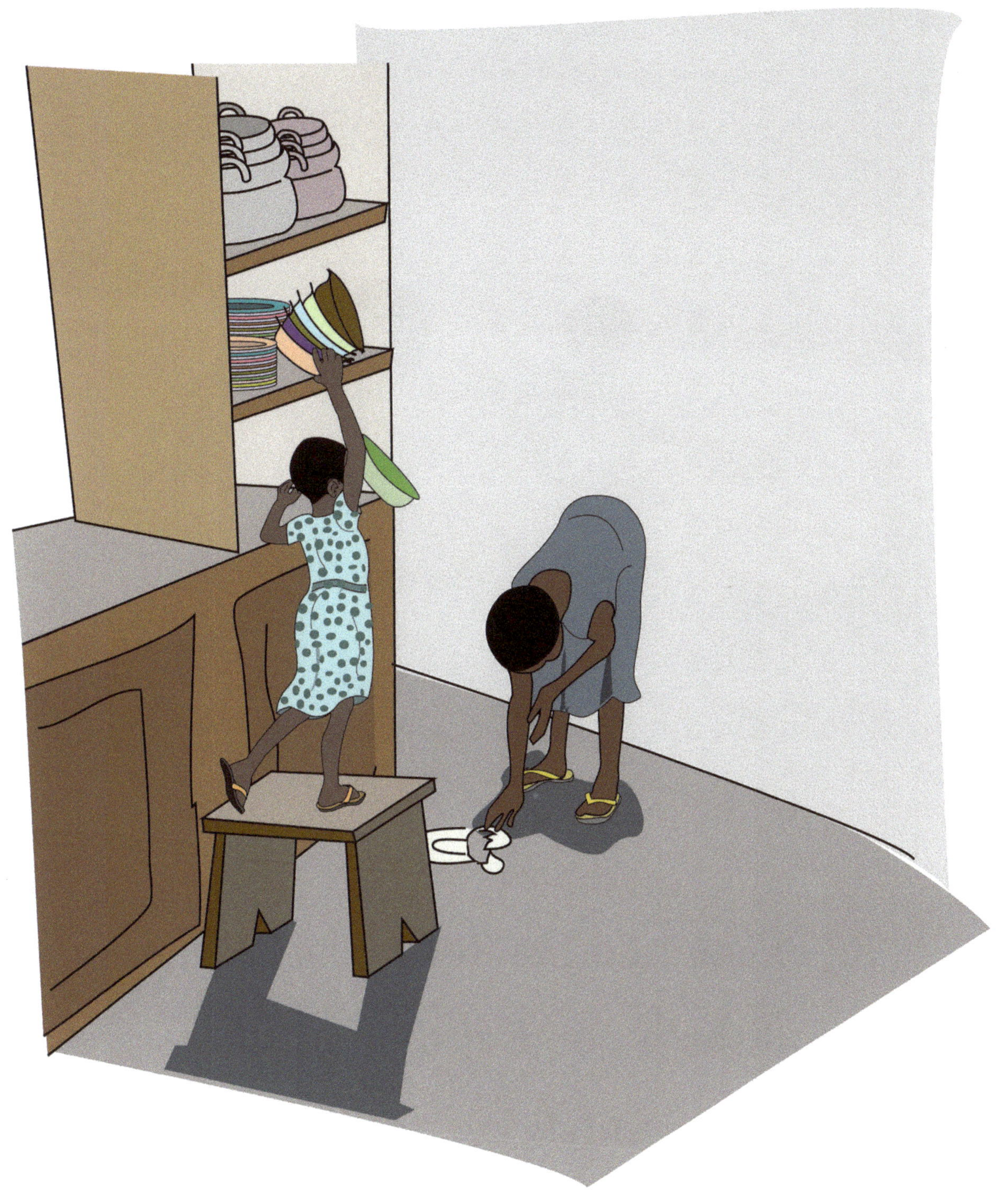

She stays out of trouble, but
I easily get in trouble!
Then she comes over to make
things better again.

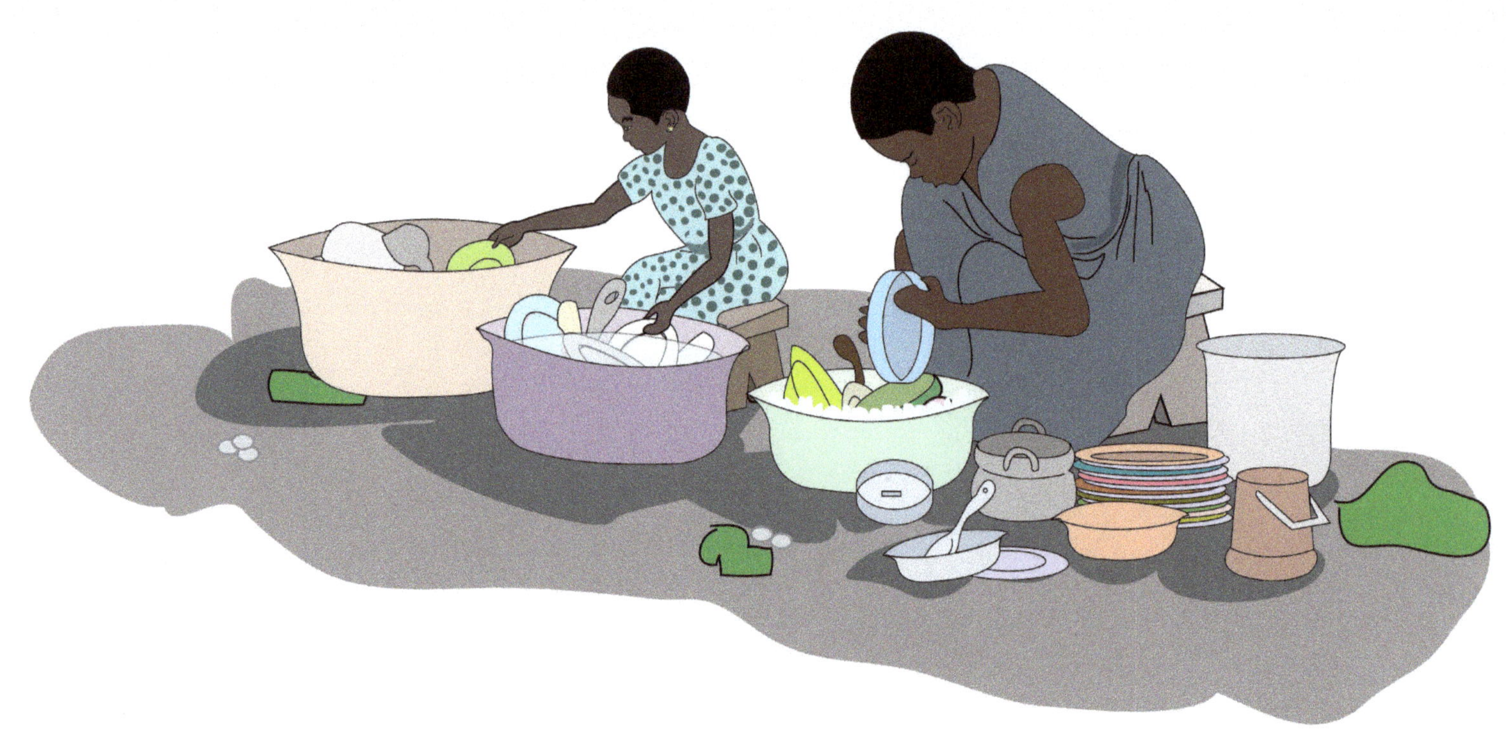

I can't do the dishes that well,
but she is good at doing dishes.
So she just lets me do the rinsing.

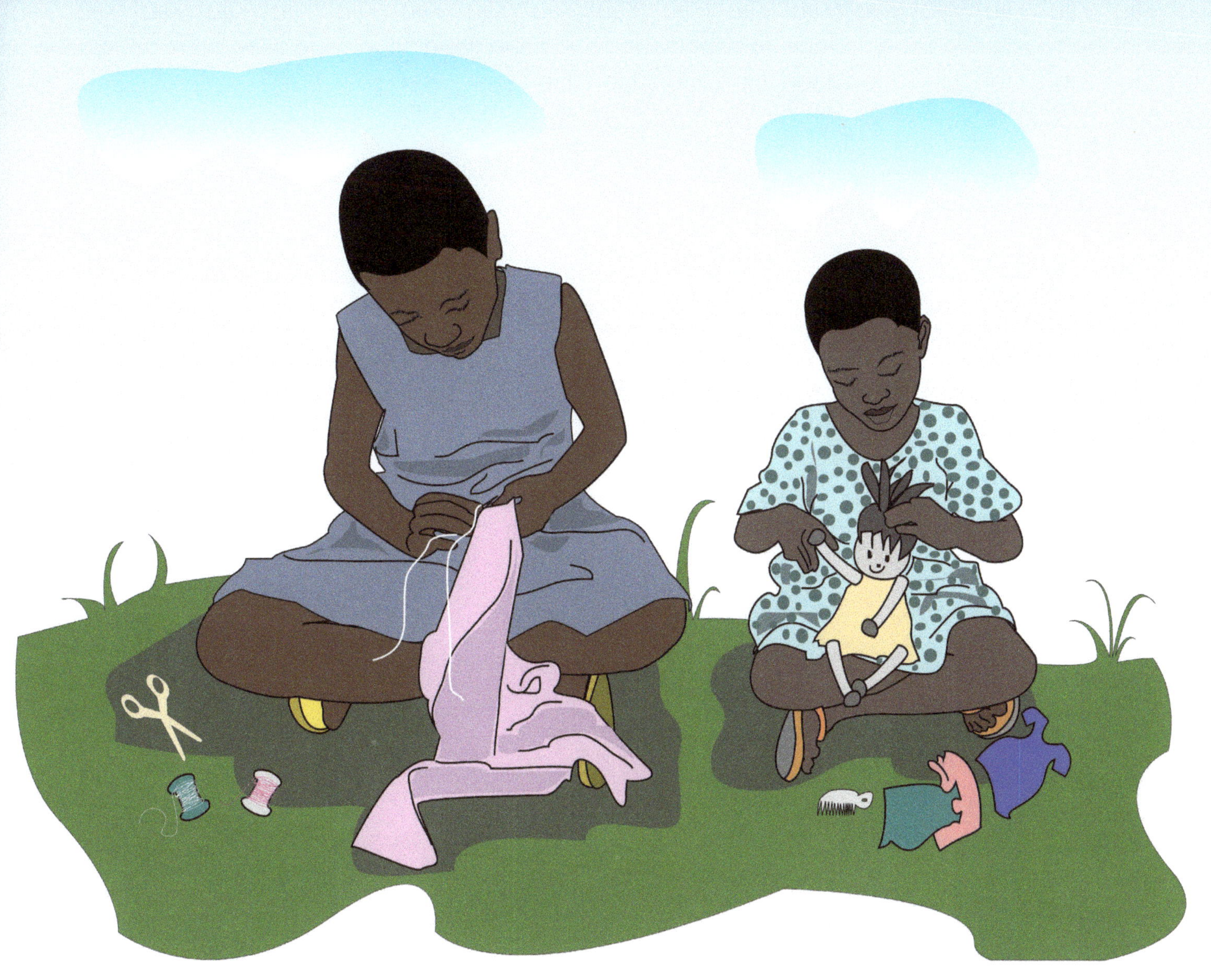

She can make doll clothing, but I can't.
So she makes doll clothing for both of our dolls.

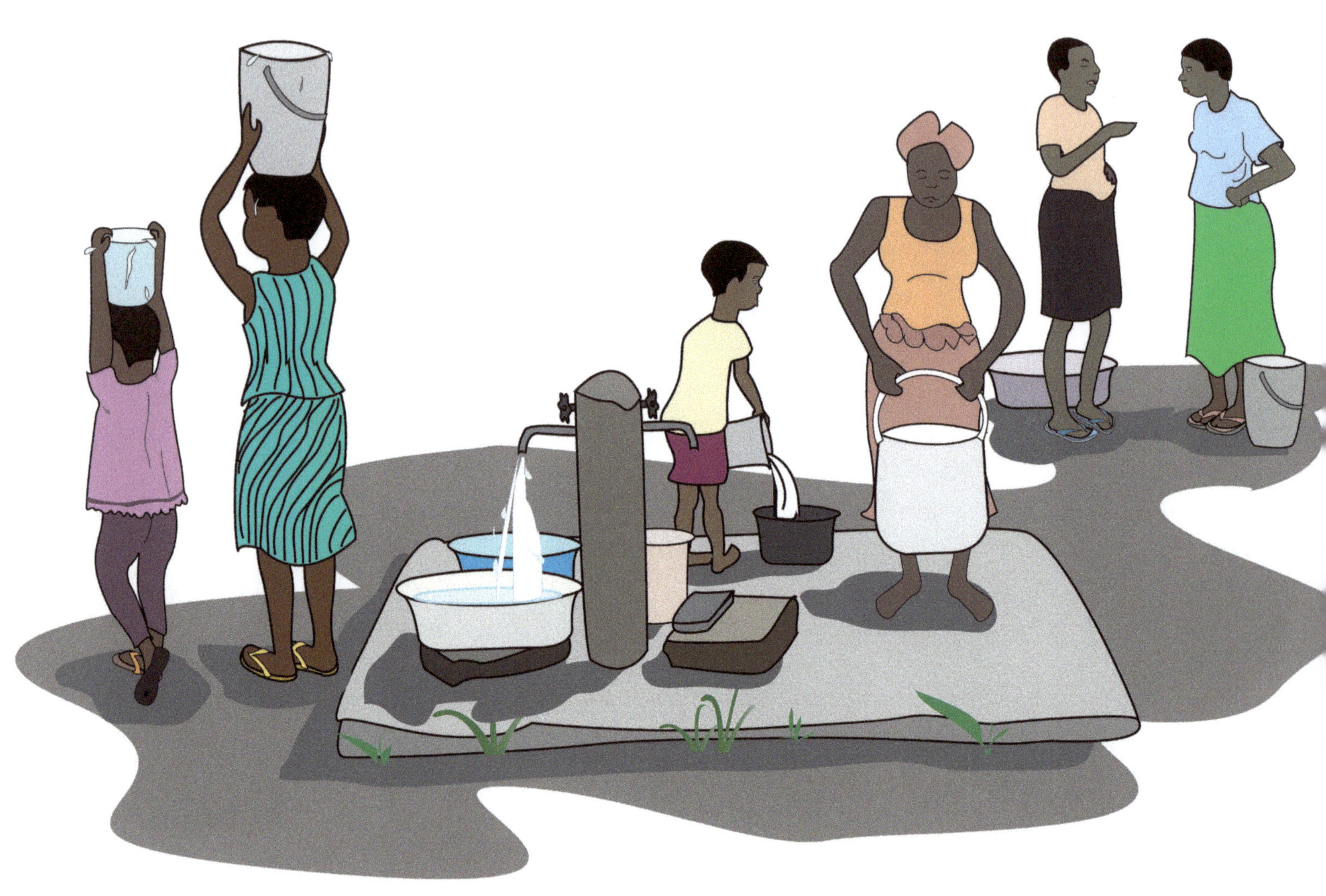

When we have to go and fetch water,
she lets me take the smaller bucket.

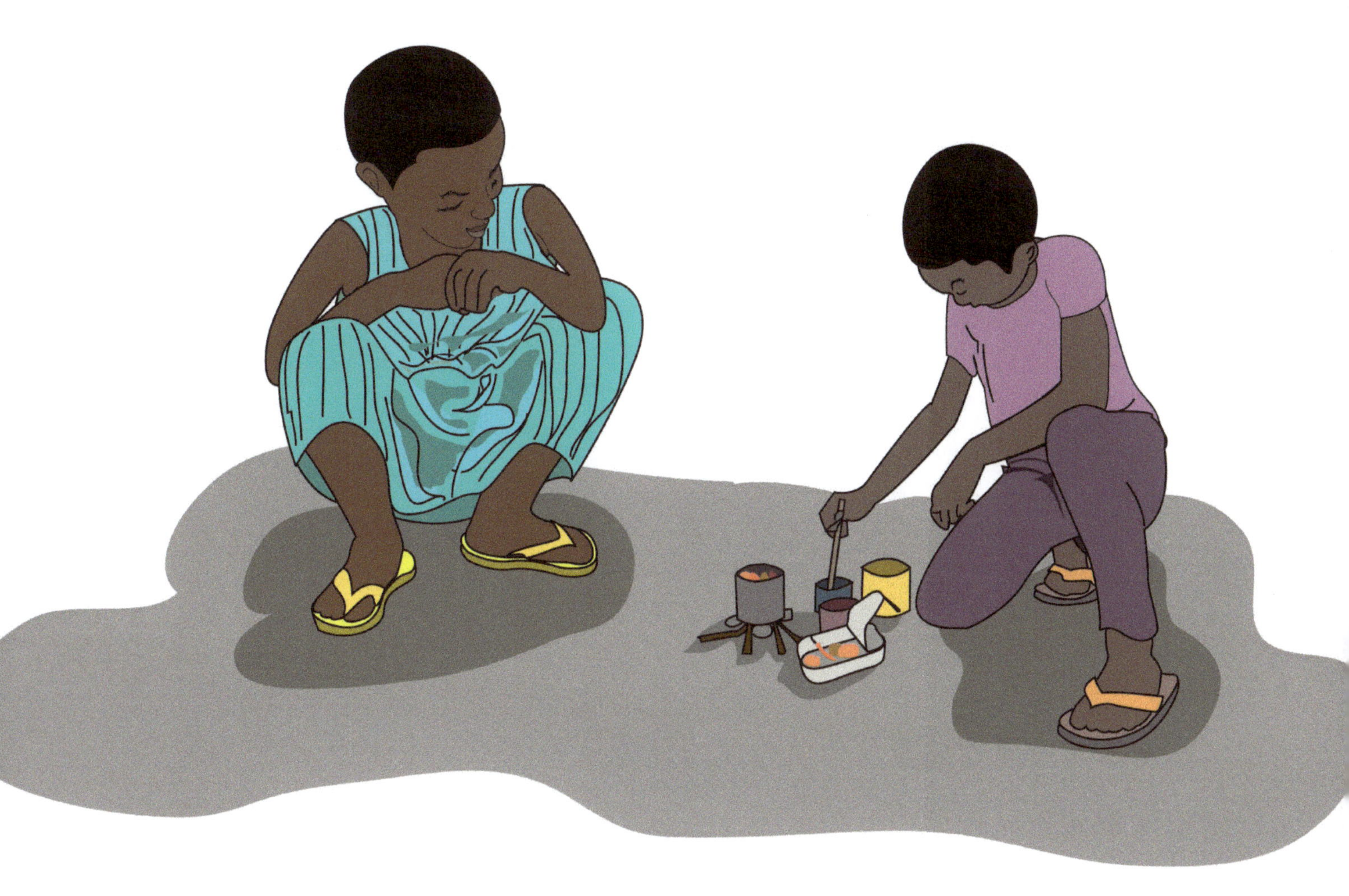

I like it when we play house together,
because she does not order me around.
We take turns doing stuff.

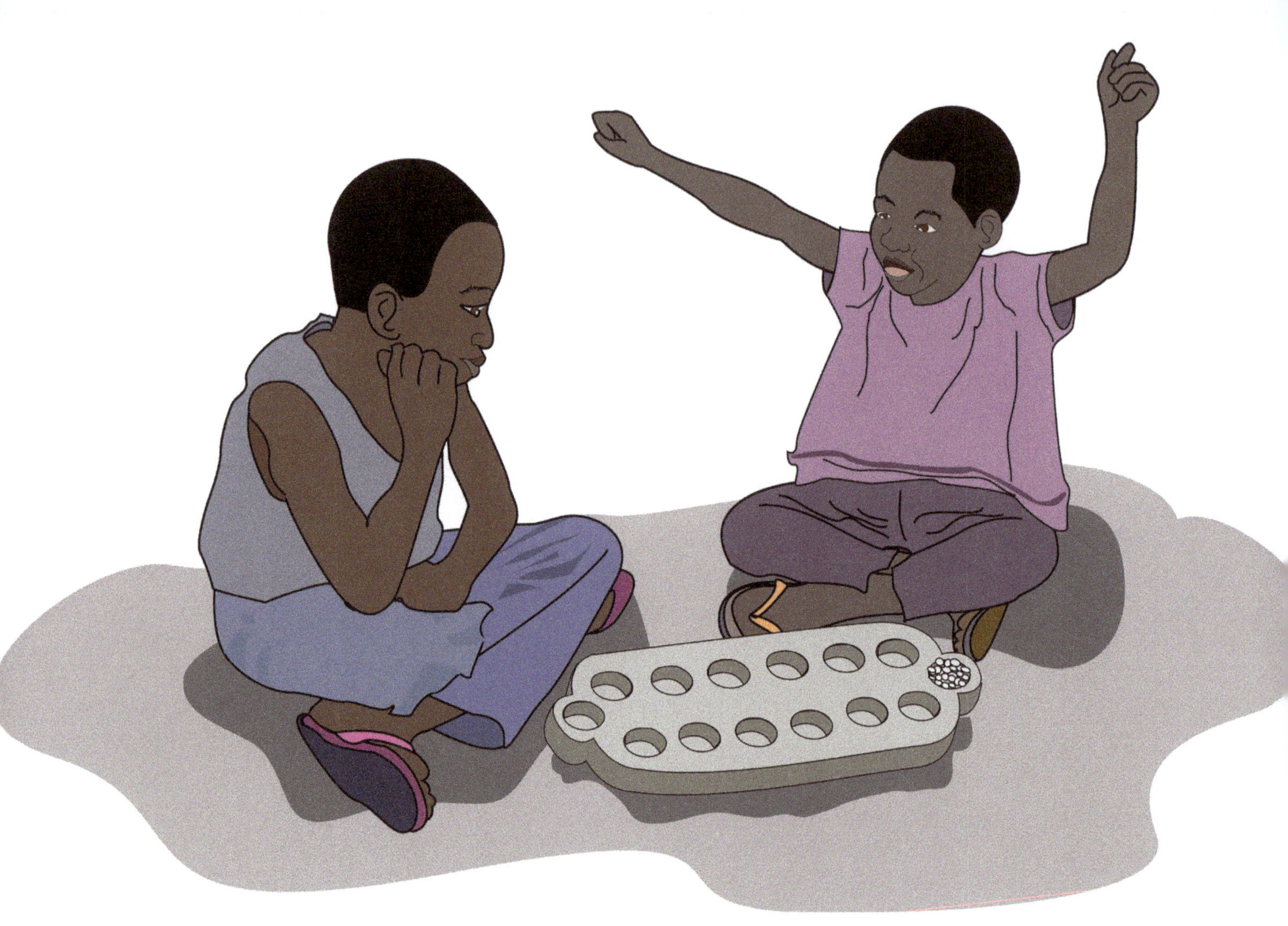

When we play games she lets me win some games,
but she wins other times too.

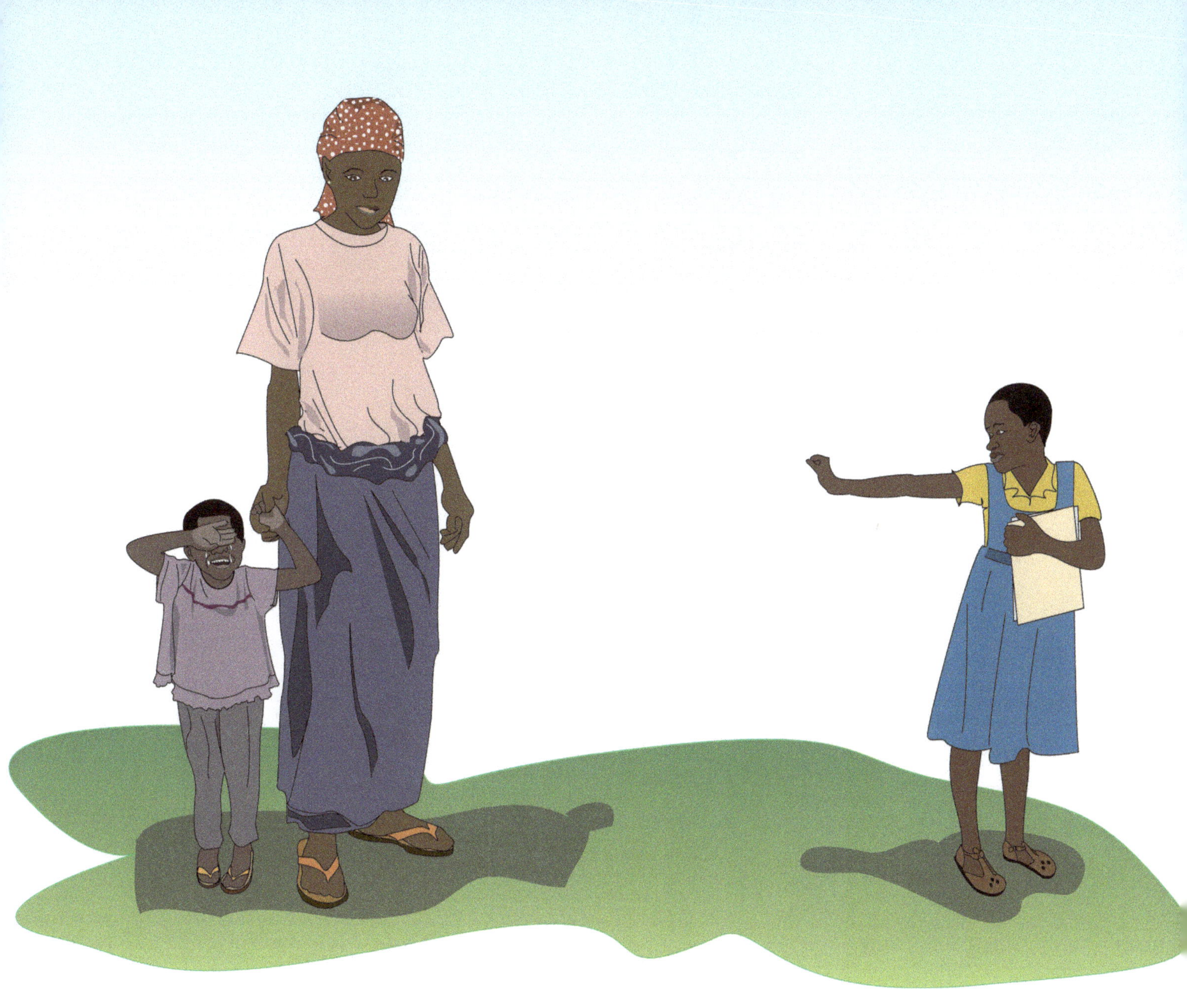

When she is ready to start kindergarten,
I want to go to school too.
I cry and cry until I am also
allowed to go to school.

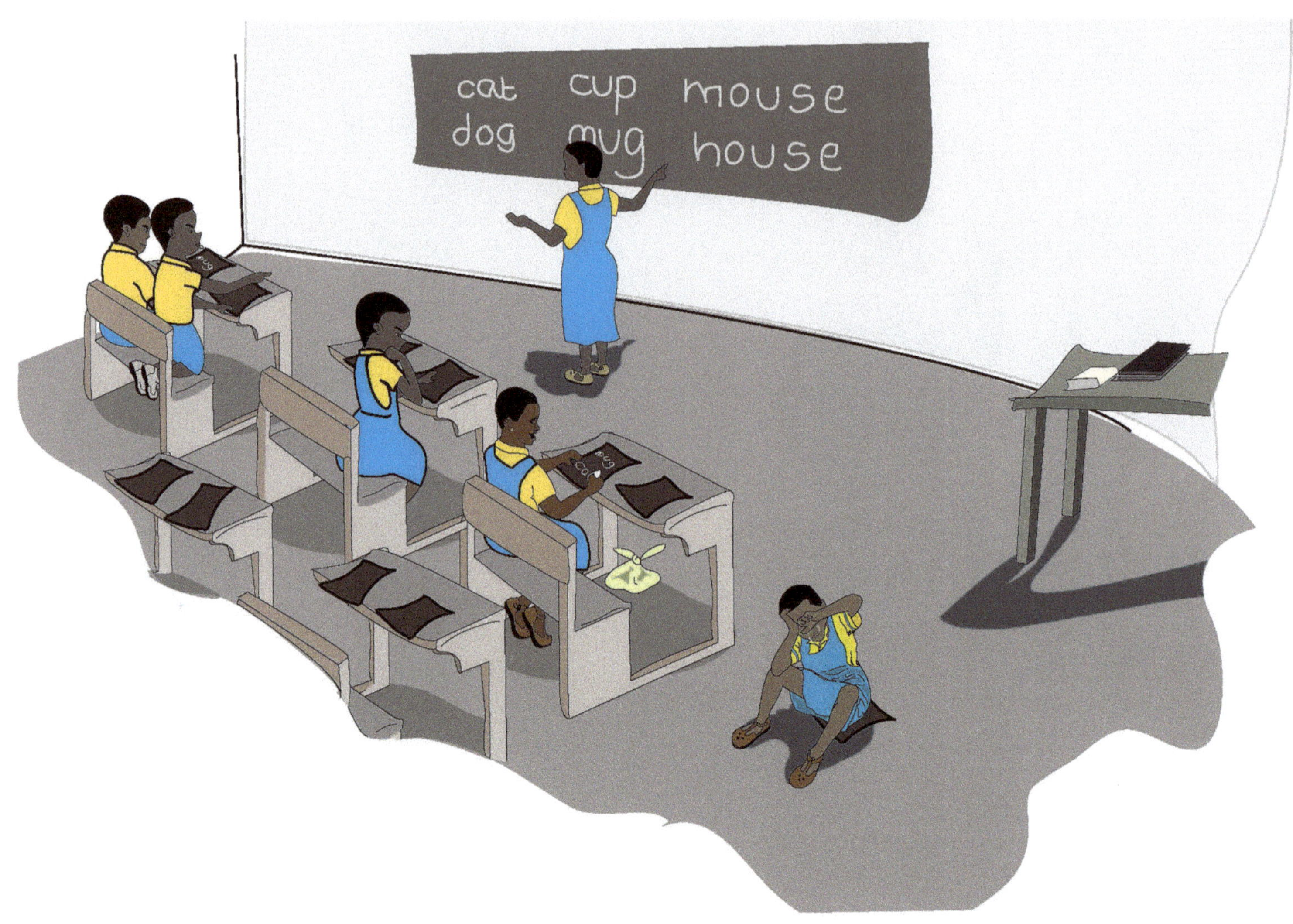

She can write her 1, 2, 3s and her A, B, Cs,
but I can't. So I sit by myself all day.

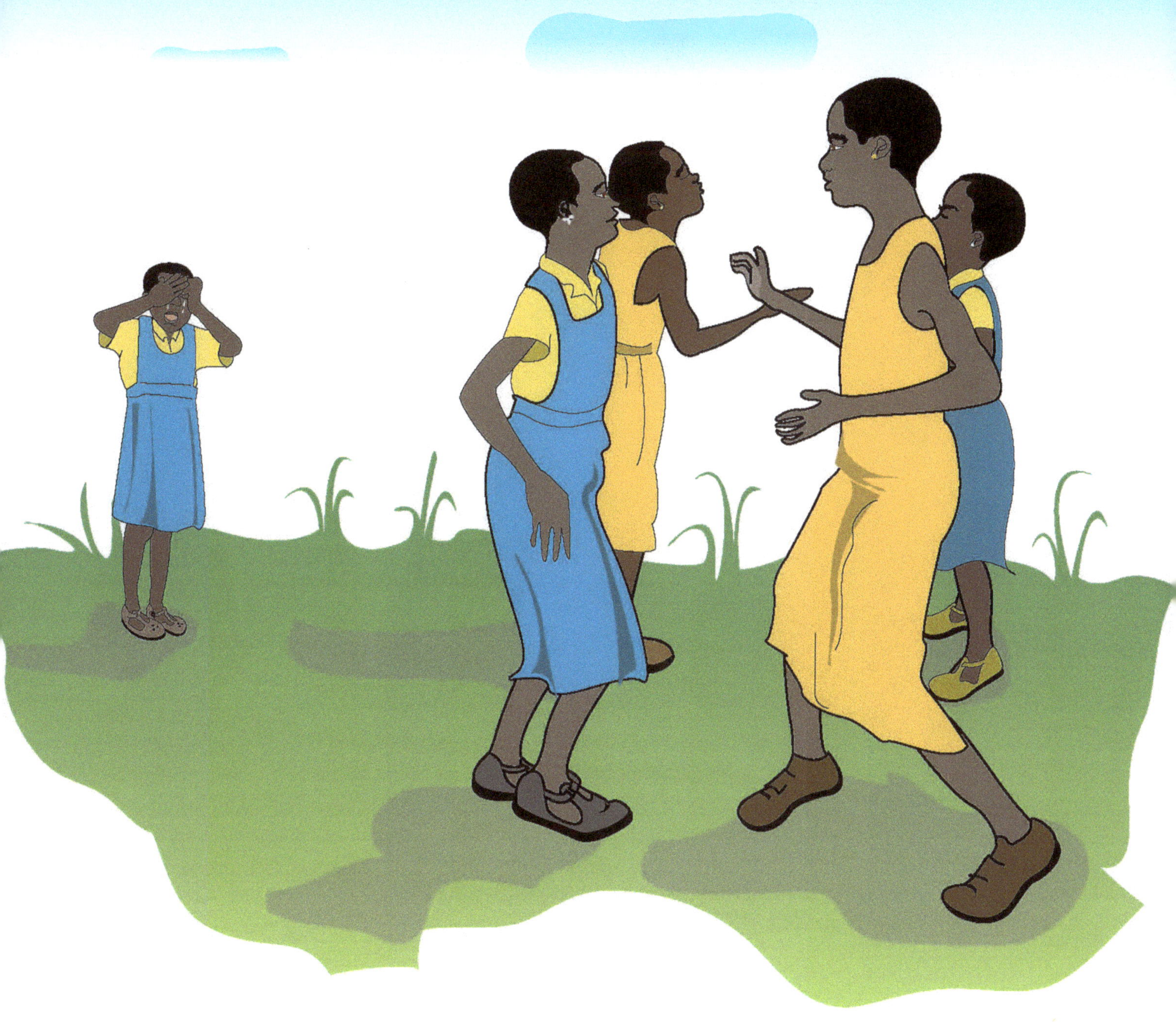

She has fun at school, but it is not fun for me.
So I cry a lot.

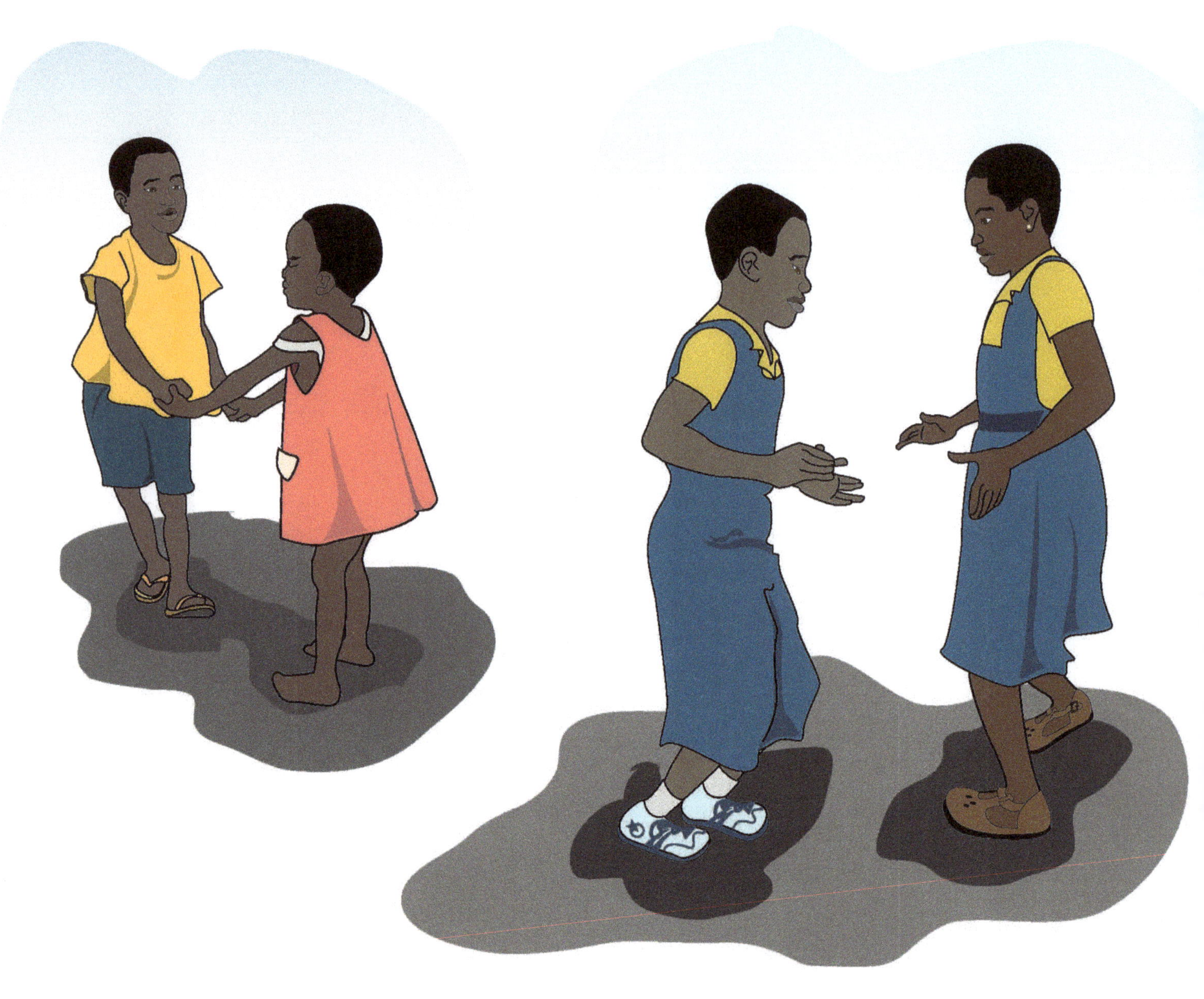

I then decide to stay home and
play while she goes to school.

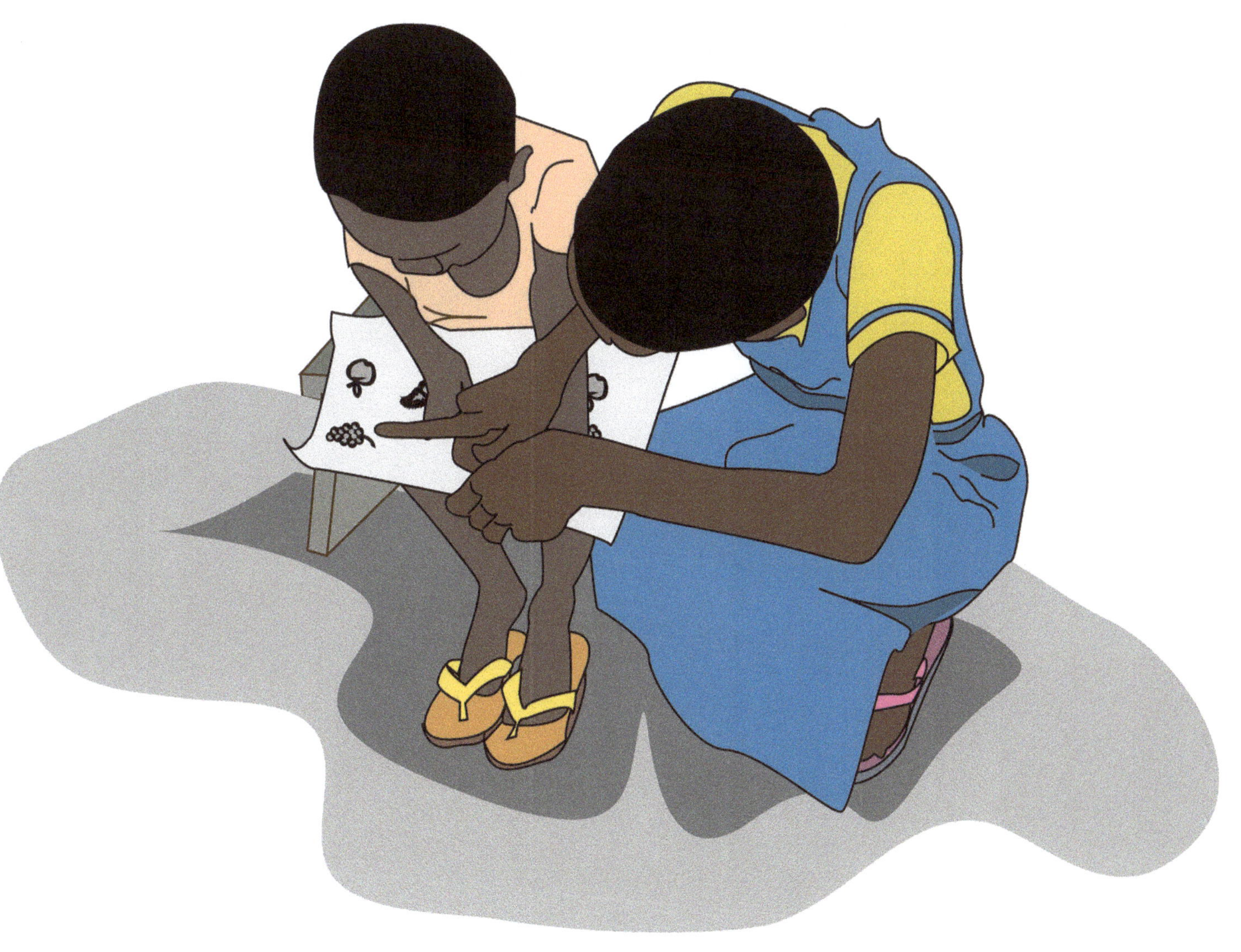

It is more fun when she comes home
from school and teaches me some of the
games and songs she has learned.

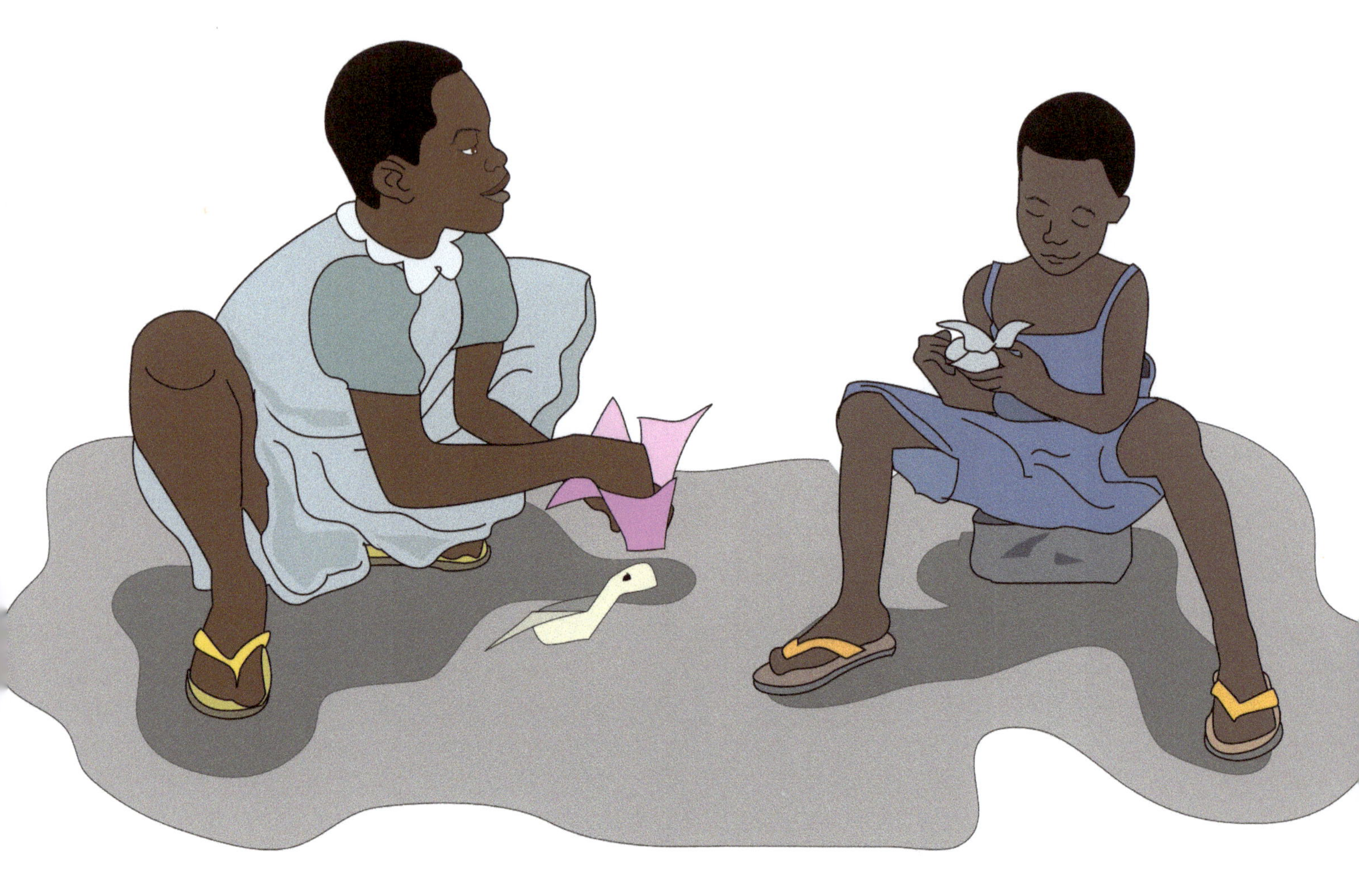

She lets me play with the things
she makes at school.

She teaches me how to make some of them, too.

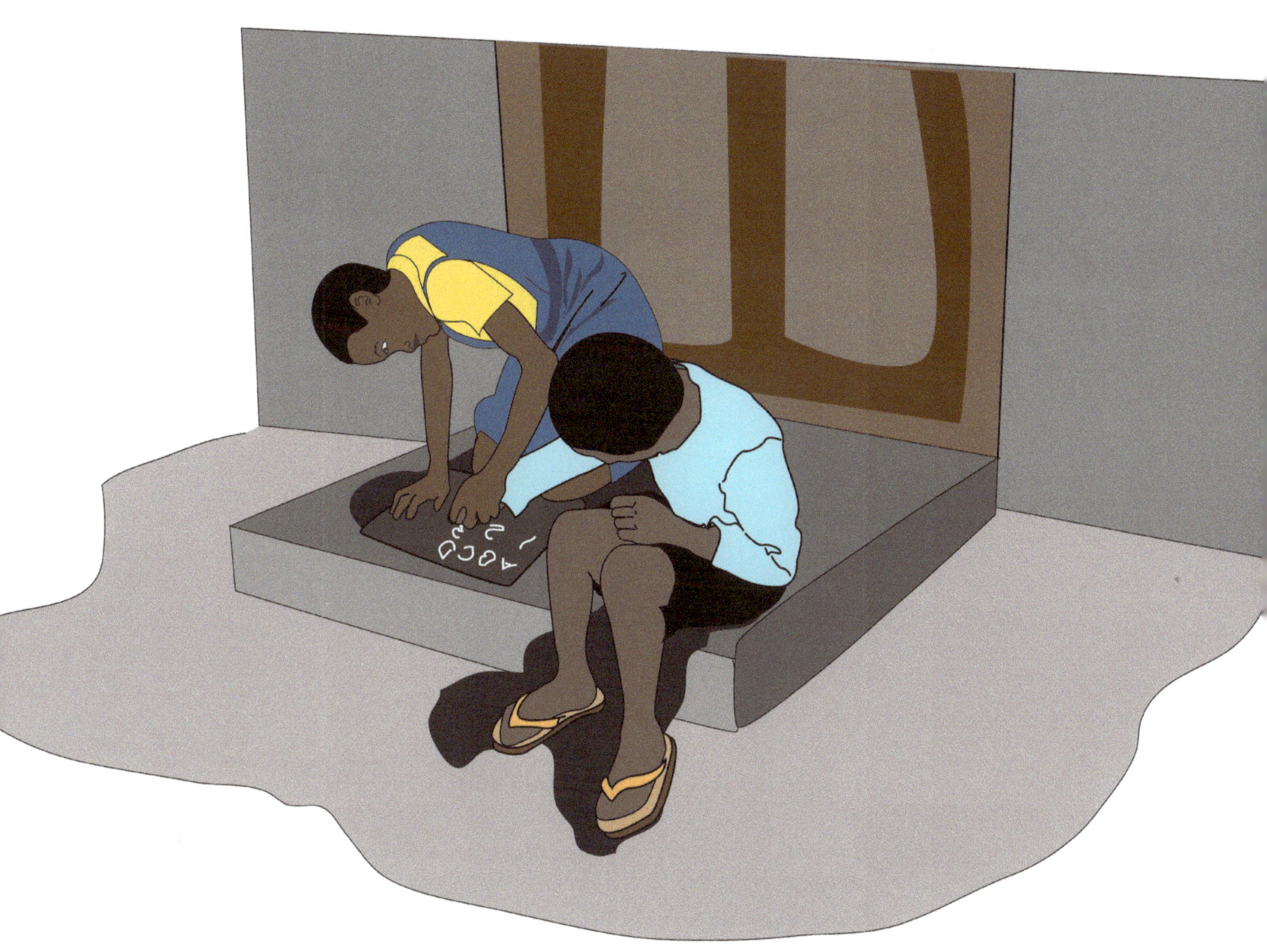

She teaches me how to write 1, 2, 3s and A, B, Cs when we play school.

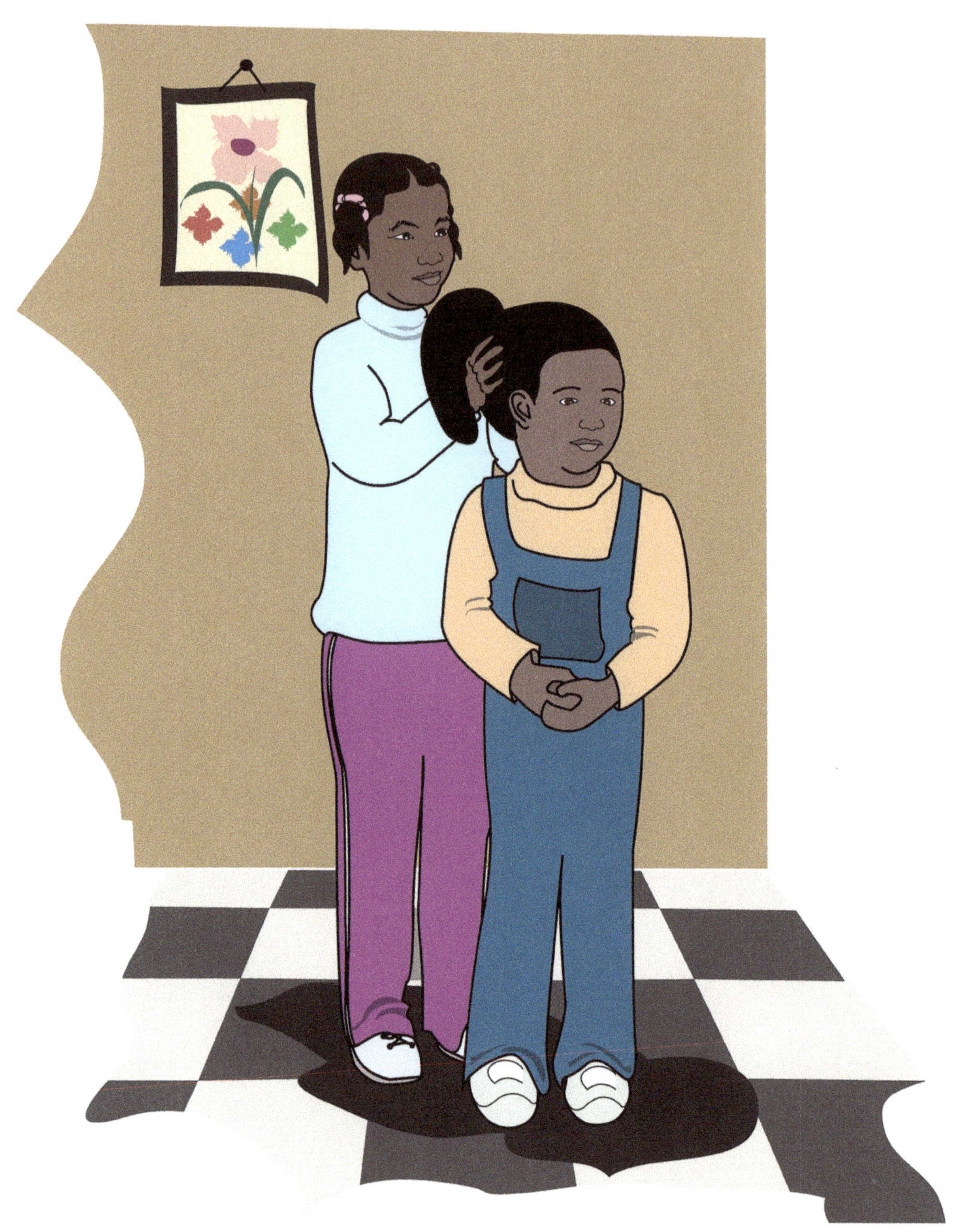

Do you have a sister?

Do you play with her?

Do you help her out?

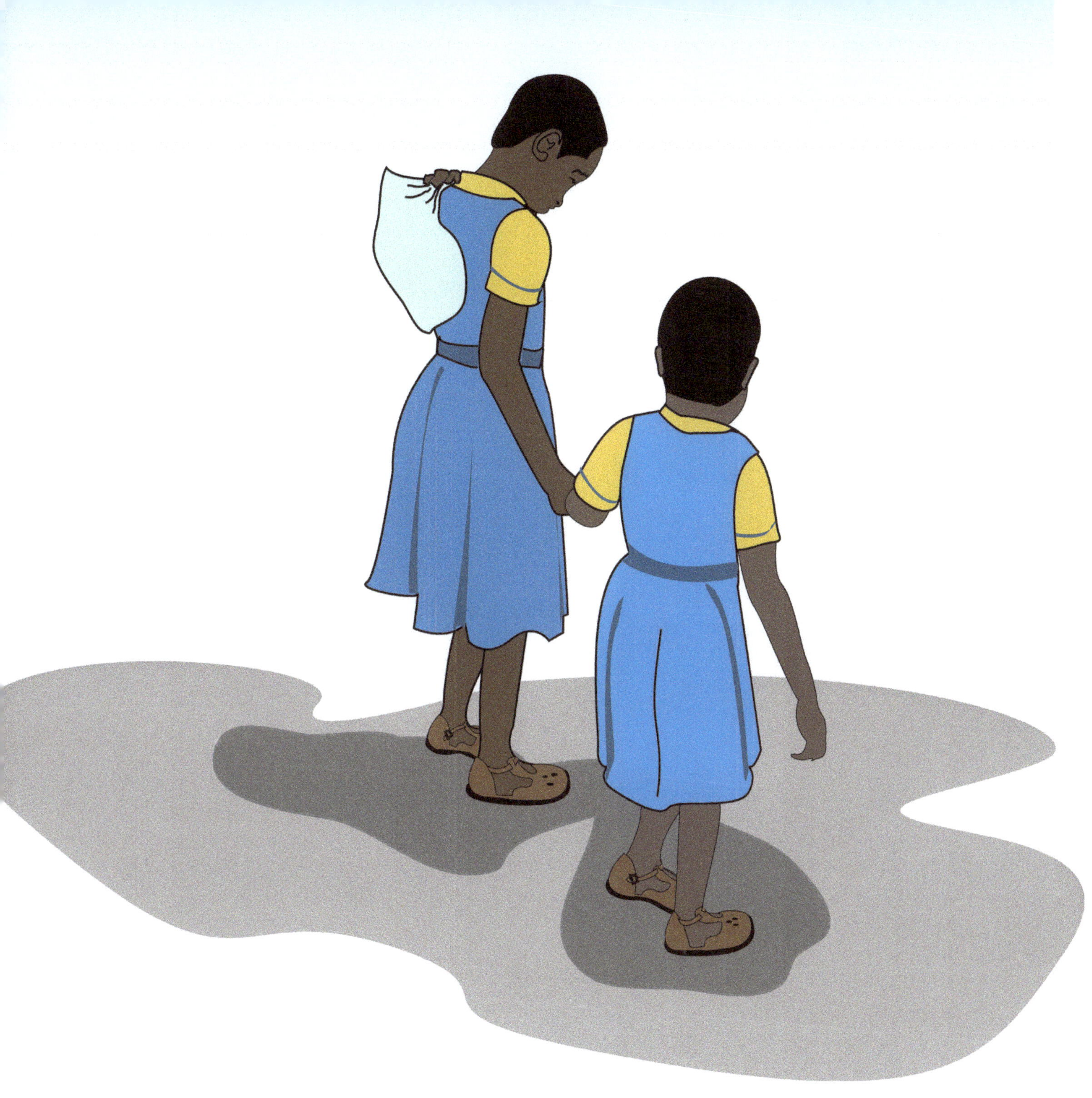

You can be a sister and a best friend to her.

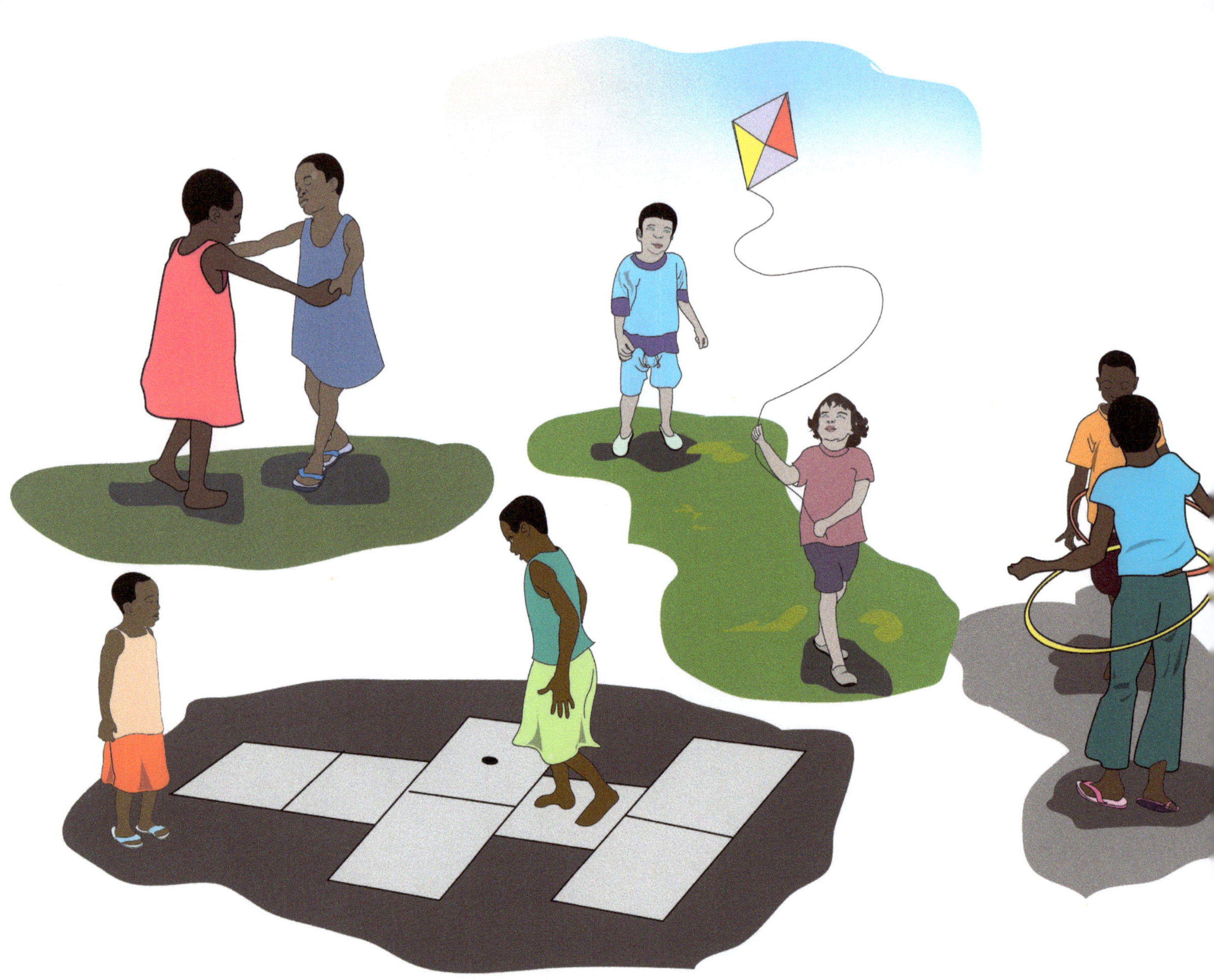

Do you have a brother?
Do you play with him?
Do you help him out?

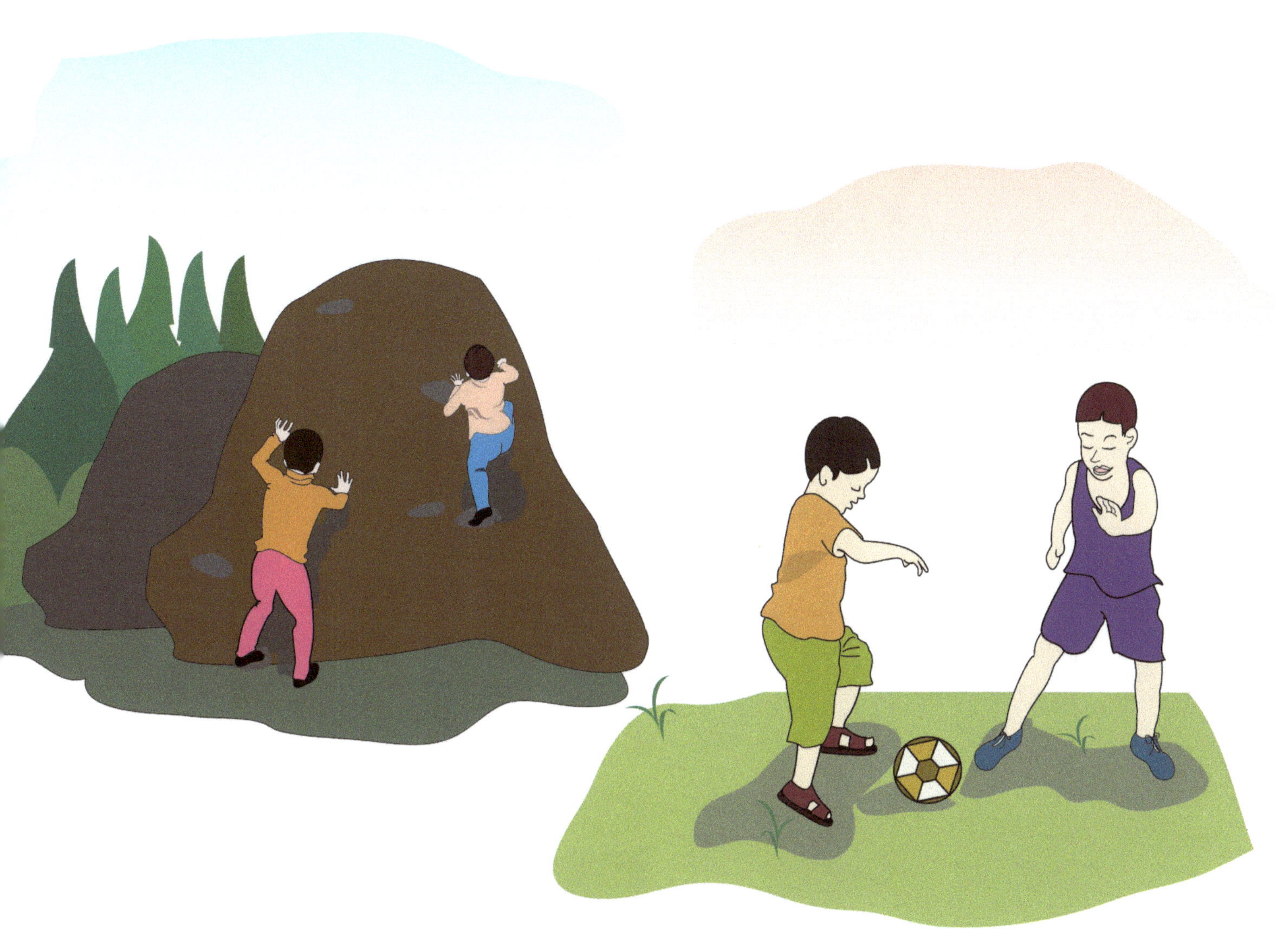

You can be a brother and a best friend to him.

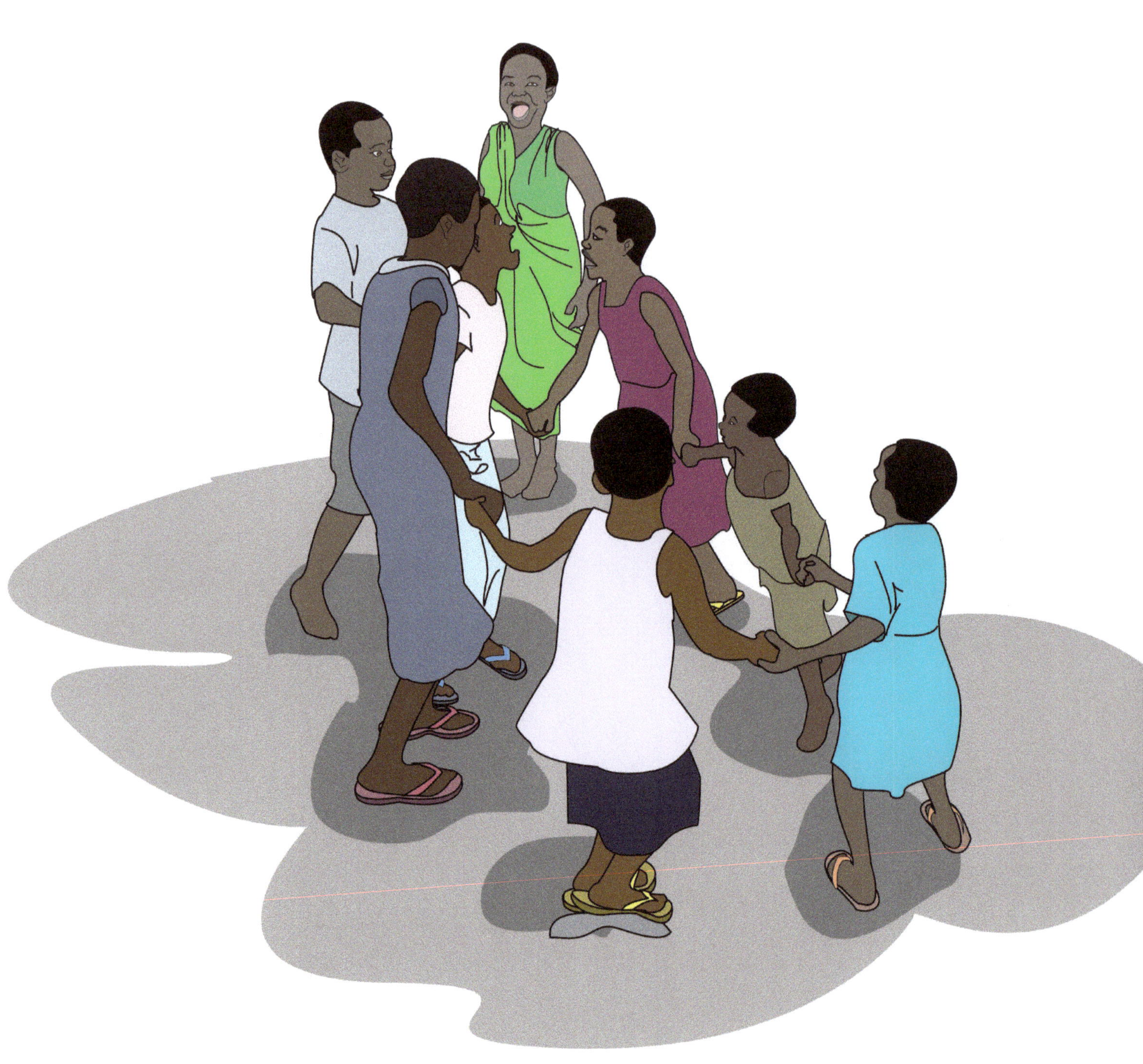

All happy and playing together.

The End